BEC
A BIBLICAL
LEADER

ENDORSEMENTS

"In this book, Jeremy approaches leadership in a holistic manner, dealing with ideas and issues that every leader needs to contemplate. Each principle is rooted in God's Word which is Jeremy's anchor throughout the book. He also gives a leadership challenge for every principle, allowing the reader to practically apply that principle to their own situation. This is a valuable resource for anyone in leadership, desiring to become the leader that God has called them to become."

DAVE LANE
Satellite Director
Youth Unlimited YFC Sarnia-Lambton

"*Becoming A Biblical Leader* is a thoughtful and practical workbook that can help both individuals and groups as they work through key thoughts about leadership. As a thirty-day daily guide, it is succinct enough to be used in a variety of settings and with a cross-section of people, helping in their foundational development as leaders."

DAVID HORITA
Pacific Region Director
Fellowship of Evangelical Baptist Churches

"Serving Christ in a northern church presents many unique challenges and joys. As seen in the life of Jesus and Paul the wilderness affords opportunity in the journey of knowing God. Pastor Jeremy Norton, in the great tradition of being formed and forming others in

Christ, has some wise and generous counsel for those serving fellow believers in the ways of God's Word. *Becoming a Biblical Leader* brings us to that far off beach where Paul and the leaders of the Ephesian church knelt down and prayed to God for the sake of Gospel and Church. May we all join them and learn something of what Jesus said concerning leadership; that it was "not so among you" as it is among the Nations. The Jesus way surely begins on our knees.

REV. DR. T. GREGORY ANDERSON
Pastor in the North

"The best leaders are always seeking ways to grow in all that it means to be a leader. Jeremy models this in his own life and now offers the wisdom he has gleaned over the years to his readers. This book is a thirty-day growth plan that offers a short daily devotional, a key portion of Scripture on which to reflect, and space to write out notes on how you will put each day's thoughts into action. Wise. Biblical. Challenging. I highly recommend it!"

DR. BARTON PRIEBE, D.MIN.
President
Northwest Seminary

BECOMING
A BIBLICAL
LEADER

30 Days of Scriptural Principle and Spiritual Growth

Jeremy Norton

AMBASSADOR INTERNATIONAL
GREENVILLE, SOUTH CAROLINA & BELFAST, NORTHERN IRELAND

www.ambassador-international.com

Becoming a Biblical Leader
30 Days of Scriptural Principle and Spiritual Growth

Hardcover ISBN: 978-1-64960-592-4
Paperback ISBN: 978-1-64960-504-7
eISBN: 978-1-64960-548-1

Edited by Kimberly Davis
Cover design by Hannah Linder Designs
Interior typesetting by Dentelle Design

AMBASSADOR INTERNATIONAL
Emerald House Group, Inc.
411 University Ridge, Suite B14
Greenville, SC 29601
United States
www.ambassador-international.com

AMBASSADOR BOOKS
The Mount
2 Woodstock Link
Belfast, BT6 8DD
Northern Ireland, United Kingdom
www.ambassadormedia.co.uk

The colophon is a trademark of Ambassador, a Christian publishing company.

TABLE OF CONTENTS

AUTHOR'S NOTE

Being confident of this, that he who began a good work in you will
carry it on to completion until the day of Christ Jesus.

—Philippians 1:6

Over the past few decades, I've been growing as a leader. Growing is all about seasons. A lot of work takes place before we can reap a harvest, which is why embracing biblical leadership is so critical for growth and even more critical for the leader whose desire is to lead well. I want my leadership to encompass every role and responsibility in my life. I want to lead well as a husband and a father. I want to lead well as the pastor and shepherd of a local church. I want to lead well in my community and in every day-to-day interaction I may have.

I firmly feel God's calling on my life to become a person who leads from a biblical foundation. Furthermore, I believe that Scriptures like Philippians 1:6 confirm that any call God placed upon us will be carried out—not for self-glorification but for His glory and the blessing of others. That said, it's important to note that I have not yet arrived. I'm growing, and growth has its share of ups and downs. Day in and day out, I make many errors of judgment. My character flaws continue to trip me up and prevent me from achieving what God has called me to be. Nevertheless, every fall that I've experienced has been followed by a season of growth. Each failure has taught me an invaluable truth about myself.

My personal mission statement continually brings me back to my calling: "serving Christ by cultivating biblical leadership through writing, equipping, and communications." This mission statement can be organized into five steps of importance and facilitation:

1. Serving Christ in every aspect of my life
2. Cultivating biblical leadership as I serve
3. Writing a record of lessons and experiences
4. Equipping future leaders for growth
5. Communicating to spread the Gospel

Regardless of your position in leadership, this book will provide a thirty-day opportunity to focus on your calling as a biblical leader. In turn, you will experience the growth you need to truly lead well.

In His Service,

Pastor Jeremy Norton

HAVE MORE FAITH

Now faith is confidence in what we hope for and assurance about
what we do not see. This is what the ancients were commended for.

—Hebrews 11:1-2

It's easy to get caught up in the events of the day. So many tasks and responsibilities can distract us from what's important. Where does faith fit into our day? Should faith flow through every facet, or should we set aside a certain time of the day? Should faith be constant or a specific focus?

Hebrews 11 begins, "Now faith is being sure of what we hope for and certain of what we do not see. This is what the ancients were commended for" (vs. 1-2). Following this statement, the author uses an array of Old Testament forefathers to illustrate the exemplary faith that was demonstrated throughout their lives. These leaders were not recognized for their bravery nor their ability to coordinate people and projects. No, it was their *faith* that was the commendable attribute!

At the end of our lives, we should all want to hear the words, "Well done, good and faithful servant" (Matt. 25:21a). A great leader must not simply have faith but have such faith as to be commended. Therefore, we should not simply work through our day without clinging to some faith-based perspective and ongoing position or attribute.

Leadership Challenge: Read Hebrews 11

Consider the possibility that faith could be one of your commendable character traits and get serious about making faith a key part of your day. Set reminders to apply faith to key projects on which you work or into the lives of the people with whom you work. Bring faith into your daily life.

NOTES

_____

_____

_____

_____

_____

_____

_____

_____

_____

_____

_____

_____

_____

Day 2
SPEAK WITH AUTHORITY

*Therefore I want you to know that God's salvation has been sent to
the Gentiles, and they will listen!*

—Acts 28:28

We've all been in the pressure cooker of debates and heated discussions over various important and less-than-important issues. They can take a serious toll on our time and energy. Speaking with clarity and authority always improves our ability to find a solution; however, if the discussion is going nowhere, sometimes speaking with authority means knowing when to end the debate.

Paul was a great leader who knew that time was short. He understood his role and his mission, part of which was preaching to the Jewish leaders. In Acts 28, we find him in a showdown with these men. Some of them believe Paul's claims of Jesus' being the Messiah are true, while some deny his teaching. To offer authoritative evidence, Paul uses prophetic words familiar to the Jews. Nevertheless, many of the leaders stand firm in their disbelief. Paul has no choice but to end the debate with this statement: "Therefore I want you to know that God's salvation has been sent to the Gentiles, and they will listen" (v. 28).

Like Paul, we need to accept when our efforts are not producing fruit. If a conversation no longer benefits the situation, it's time to end it before damage is done.

Leadership Challenge: Read Acts 28

Consider your current work environment and the debates that steal your time and energy. Meditate in prayer over these discussions. Make specific notes in your calendar on end the conversations at your next meeting. Be bold and speak with authority on why these discussions must be brought to a close.

NOTES

_____

_____

_____

_____

_____

_____

_____

_____

_____

_____

_____

_____

_____

_____

_____

_____

_____

_____

_____

_____

_____

_____

_____

_____

_____

_____

_____

_____

_____

_____

_____

_____

_____

_____

_____

_____

_____

CHOOSE TO ACT

Then the disciple whom Jesus loved said to Peter, "It is the Lord!" As soon
as Simon Peter heard him say, "It is the Lord," he wrapped his outer
garment around him (for he had taken it off) and jumped into the water.

—John 21:7

Certain times in our lives require patience, and waiting on the Lord is the wise decision. At times, however, leaders face situations that require immediate action—especially when showing our commitment to the Lord.

The last chapter of John describes an occasion when Peter couldn't help but jump into action. This decision showed both his devotion to Christ and why he was the right leader upon which the Church should be founded. As soon as John says, "It is the Lord" (21:7), Peter throws on his outer garment, jumps out of the boat, and begins to swim to shore. Sure, the boat would eventually get there, but Peter knew that swimming would bring him face to face with his Lord that much sooner.

So many times, we play it safe. We know we need to take the initiative but tell ourselves, "It'll be uncomfortable! We might get hurt! It's not our regular game plan!" Does any of that really matter? If you've been at a standstill over a particular topic or issue for this long, will it feel different tomorrow? Next week? A year from now? It might just be time to act!

Leadership Challenge: Read John 21

Is today the day you do something Peter-like? Maybe you have been hearing the Lord leading in a certain direction, but you have put off making your move. Spend time in prayer. Then simply choose to act and take that first step of forward motion.

NOTES

_____

_____

_____

_____

_____

_____

_____

_____

_____

_____

_____

_____

_____

_____

_____

_____

_____

_____

_____

_____

_____

_____

_____

_____

_____

_____

_____

_____

_____

_____

_____

_____

_____

_____

_____

_____

_____

_____

Day 4
REMEMBER THE PAST

Tell them that the flow of the Jordan was cut off before the ark of the covenant of the Lord. When it crossed the Jordan, the waters of the Jordan were cut off. These stones are to be a memorial to the people of Israel forever.

—Joshua 4:7

Christians often associate good memories with God's faithfulness, such as a time when He carried us through a trial or difficult circumstance. Should we not do something to preserve these memories and, perhaps, pass them down to our children?

In the Bible, we read about Joshua, a great leader who was courageous and full of faith. He had no doubt whether God would fulfill His promises, and by God's hand, Joshua guided God's people through many trials. In Joshua 3, God miraculously led Israel through the Jordan River. In chapter four, God instructed the people to "take up twelve stones from the middle of the Jordan . . . put them down at the place where you stay tonight" (4:3). He then declared that "these stones are to be a memorial to the people of Israel forever" (4:7). How did they get the stones from the middle of the Jordan? God stopped the waters. This memorial must have been very important!

Now, God may not have stopped a raging river for you, but I am sure He's brought you through some trial or difficulty. What will serve as a memorial for that time in your life—a photo, video, journal entry, blog post? How will you look back at God's faithfulness and share it with the next generation?

Leadership Challenge: Read Joshua 3 and 4

Think about the past year. What amazing trial did God help you overcome, or what difficulty did He strengthen you to endure? Prayerfully reflect on that season and thank God for His faithfulness. Then create a memorial to help you remember the past and share your story with others.

NOTES

_____

_____

_____

_____

_____

_____

_____

_____

_____

_____

_____

_____

_____

_____

_____

_____

_____

_____

_____

_____

_____

_____

_____

_____

_____

_____

_____

_____

_____

_____

_____

_____

_____

_____

_____

_____

_____

_____

_____

Day 5
SLOW YOUR ANGER

*My dear brothers and sisters, take note of this: Everyone should be
quick to listen, slow to speak and slow to become angry, because
human anger does not produce the righteousness that God desires.*

—James 1:19-20

Being quick to listen and slow to speak seem to be more difficult
for some people than others. An introvert may be contemplative
and listen to all the details before giving an opinion. An extrovert
may have to exert serious focus to hold an opinion while listening
to others first. Regardless of the personality types involved,
conversations can quickly turn into arguments, unless everyone
receives a fair opportunity to participate in the discussion. Introverts
may shut down; extroverts may lash out; but anger is not specific to
personality. We all stop listening, get angry, and react at some point.

James gives us great wisdom to this topic: to "be quick to listen,
slow to speak" (1:19). But he does not end there. The second part of
this Scripture completes the thought. We need to be "slow to become
angry, because human anger does not produce the righteousness that
God desires" (1:19-20). Some people will always be ready to give an
opinion, rather than to listen. Some people will ignore everyone else

and do their own thing. We should be cautious in choosing anger as a solution, despite our frustration.

Leadership Challenge: Read James 1

Concentrate prayer on recent conversations you have had. Have you given too many opinions or blocked out others? Has anger stirred inside you? Consider how you can improve these interactions and set goals to do so. Place a date beside each goal and look for opportunities to slow yourself, release anger, and humbly enact your plan. You might just make it through the conversation, rekindle a friendship, or develop a new one.

NOTES

_____

_____

_____

_____

_____

_____

_____

_____

_____

_____

_____

_____

Day 6
MEMORIZE A VERSE

Being confident of this, that he who began a good work in you will
carry it on to completion until the day of Christ Jesus.

—Philippians 1:6

A leader's life is full of trials. A Christian leader's faith is constantly tested, as we navigate our ministries through this chaotic world. Though we have hope for eternity, life does not get easier.

During the conversion experience or soon after trusting Jesus, many Christians connect with a particular passage or verse. Some refer to it as a life verse because it is pivotal in understanding God's plan for their salvation. This verse is typically the first to be memorized and often brought to mind in times of doubt and struggle.

Philippians 1:6 is such a verse for me. It has guided me through many a trial and temptation. Whenever I feel like I cannot move forward, this verse tells me I can. I must be confident because Christ "began a good work in [me and He] will carry it on to completion." He started it, and He is faithful to complete it!

Memorizing this single verse had a huge influence on my life. Maybe you have had a similar experience with a particular verse or passage. Focus on that Scripture today.

Leadership Challenge: Read your
favorite chapter of Scripture

Which verse has had the greatest influence on your life? Write it in a journal or enter it in a notes app. Spend time in prayerful thanksgiving as you consider what God has done for you through this verse. As God brings thoughts to mind, create a bullet point for each situation under the verse. Following your time of prayer, you will have a detailed, personal account of how memorizing a single verse can have a lasting effect on your life and leadership.

NOTES

_____

_____

_____

_____

_____

_____

_____

_____

_____

_____

_____

_____

_____

_____

Day 7
TRUST GOD'S LEADERSHIP

Your rulers are rebels, partners with thieves; they all love bribes and
chase after gifts. They do not defend the cause of the fatherless; the
widow's case does not come before them.

—Isaiah 1:23

Typically, a leadership position is given when a degree of trust is proven or earned. Unfortunately, sometimes people change once that position has been bestowed. All of a sudden, trust begins to fade. In the first chapter of Isaiah, God gives the prophet a vision with a message for such leaders. In verse twenty-three, God says, "Your rulers are rebels, partners with thieves; they all love bribes and chase after gifts. They do not defend the cause of the fatherless; the widow's case does not come before them." Some of us have experienced this type of leadership in our workplace, our government, and even our churches!

Perhaps you are under this type of leadership right now. Maybe you are coming under the conviction of being this type of leader. It is difficult to see God's plan or understand why He would allow such poor leaders. Nevertheless, God is Sovereign. The same God Who worked out a masterful plan during Isaiah's day is still with us. We should strive to find balance, submitting to God's Sovereignty during our quest for justice.

Leadership Challenge: Read Isaiah 1

As you read this passage, consider your leadership and the leadership around you. Write down specific people and circumstances and then pray over each situation, asking God to provide the trust needed to endure and, if necessary, the action items needed to move forward.

NOTES

_____

_____

_____

_____

_____

_____

_____

_____

_____

_____

_____

_____

_____

_____

Day 8
SERVE AT HOME

But if serving the LORD seems undesirable to you, then choose for
yourselves this day whom you will serve, whether the gods your
ancestors served beyond the Euphrates, or the gods of the Amorites,
in whose land you are living. But as for me and my household, we
will serve the LORD.

—Joshua 24:15

Many leaders have served in positions with large organizations, yet neglected their servant leadership responsibilities at home. All too often, news stories break about some director, CEO, or pastor who has forsaken his family, often ending in a significant moral failure. These reports indicate that leadership should begin at home.

Joshua 24 recounts a gathering of the people to renew their commitment to God's Law. During his address, Joshua gives a phrase that has become a pillar statement for the Judeo-Christian world: "But as for me and my household, we will serve the LORD" (v. 15). Much like the people of Israel so many years ago, we have a responsibility to make this pledge.

Leaders the world over enjoy renowned status, bank accounts full of money, and thousands of followers across major social platforms. On their death beds, all of these things fade. At the gravesite, the status, money, and social media lose significance. At eternity's door, the investment made in one's family carries far more weight than a legacy of fame and fortune.

Leadership Challenge: Read Joshua 24

Try to imagine Joshua's public address being given in today's corporate or ministry world. How would you respond? Ask God to open your eyes to specific times and activities you can dedicate to having a greater testimony of servant leadership in your home. Let today be the beginning of a more strategic, home-based service to the Lord.

NOTES

_____

_____

_____

_____

_____

_____

_____

_____

_____

_____

_____

Day 9
ANSWER THE CALL

*When the angel of the L*ORD *appeared to Gideon, he said,*
"The Lord is with you, mighty warrior."

—Judges 6:12

Many times, leaders feel an inexplicable call to action toward a certain task. God can issue this call through His Word, prayer, another believer, music, art, or literature. Sometimes, it simply comes through a sudden moving of the Holy Spirit within our hearts. Unfortunately, we are sometimes reluctant and have an inner discussion with God on whether or not it was truly His calling. We want a stronger sign, like God's speaking audibly or sending an angel with a message, but history proves that only in rare instances does that take place.

In Judges 6, a soon-to-be leader named Gideon received one such call. "When the angel of the LORD appeared to Gideon, he said, 'The LORD is with you, mighty warrior'" (v. 12).

God was calling Gideon to action in a supernatural way, but Gideon still made excuses. "Pardon me, my lord . . . how can I save Israel? My clan is the weakest in Manasseh, and I am the least in my family" (v. 15).

The reality is that even if the Angel of the Lord visited us, most of us would take Gideon's approach. We would likely give an assortment of excuses on why we should not have been chosen to perform such a task or duty. Instead, leaders should automatically answer the call to action.

Leadership Challenge: Read Judges 6 and 7

Think about Gideon's unlikely candidacy for leadership. Yet God called him to action. Prayerfully consider how God has prompted you. Which pursuits have you avoided? As you pray, make note of the next steps necessary to answer your call.

NOTES

_____

_____

_____

_____

_____

_____

_____

_____

_____

_____

_____

_____

_____

_____

Day 10
FOLLOW GOD'S INSTRUCTION

But now your kingdom will not endure; the Lord has sought out
a man after his own heart and appointed him ruler of his people,
because you have not kept the Lord's command.

—1 Samuel 13:14

Leaders experience many days of struggle and plenty of opportunities to make mistakes, but choice is to be made within every struggle or mistake. Will we allow God to get us back on track, or will we push through arrogantly? Will we let God take control, or will we try to maintain control?

1 Samuel 13 describes the beginning of King Saul's demise as a leader. His status as king corrupted him, then he chose to neglect the proper order of sacrifice outlined by God. His struggle with patience and pride led to his downfall. Samuel brings Saul the bad news.

"You have not kept the command the Lord your God gave you; if you had, he would have established your kingdom over Israel for all time. But now your kingdom will not endure; the Lord has sought out a man after his own heart and appointed him ruler of his people, because you have not kept the Lord's command" (vs. 13b-14).

Unfortunately, King Saul's character continues to deteriorate, and God ultimately gives Saul over to his own devices. "But Samuel said

49

to him, 'I will not go back with you. You have rejected the word of
the LORD, and the LORD has rejected you as king over Israel'" (vs. 26).

Leadership Challenge: Read 1 Samuel 13 through 15

Consider Saul's opportunities to follow God's instruction and the
arrogance that prevented him from making the right decisions. What
decisions will you make today? What mistakes have you made this past
week? Ask God to bring to mind mistakes made and steps yet to be
taken. Write down His plans to make things right and move forward.

NOTES

_____

_____

_____

_____

_____

_____

_____

_____

_____

_____

_____

_____

_____

Day 11
REFRAIN FROM LUST

He had seven hundred wives of royal birth and three hundred
concubines, and his wives led him astray.

—1 Kings 11:3

Leadership can be lonely. A separation exists between a leader and the rest of the team. Yet, once in a while, a relational connection forms. It may seem harmless in the beginning, but without proper boundaries, it can turn into lustful desires. A boundary is crossed as desire develops into behavior, leading down a destructive path that costs the leader not only his career but also his family and personal integrity. In the worst-case scenario, the leader may start giving into these desires so frequently that the failure becomes habitual. The road back from that point is long and challenging!

In 1 Kings, we find a leader who fell victim to these desires and behaviors.

[King Solomon] loved many foreign women . . . Moabites, Ammonites, Edomites, Sidonians and Hittites. They were from nations about which the Lord had told the Israelites, "You must not intermarry with them, because they will surely turn your hearts after their gods." Nevertheless,

Solomon held fast to them in love. He had seven hundred wives of royal birth and three hundred concubines, and his wives led him astray (1 Kings 11:1-3).

Solomon's lustful desires turned into a habitual problem, which eventually pulled him away from his role as king. God requested that Solomon lead the people of Israel, but Solomon was more concerned with personal pleasure than curbing his lustful appetite.

Leadership Challenge: Read 1 Kings 11

Note how Solomon's lust pulled him away from obeying God. Spend time in prayer, asking God to reveal your desires for connection. Are they appropriate? Are they based on loneliness or lust? Could they be dangerous in the future? Make prayer-filled notes on how you can reroute or end harmful connections today.

NOTES

_____

_____

_____

_____

_____

_____

_____

_____

_____

INFLUENCE YOUR TEAM

After that, he poured water into a basin and began to wash his disciples'
feet, drying them with the towel that was wrapped around him.

—John 13:5

Is it better for a leader to have power or influence? Businesses acquire financial power by producing goods and services that people need or want. Governments garner political power via promises and actions that align with a particular value system. Although this scope of influence prevails for a time, it rarely endures.

In John 13, Jesus shows us how to achieve lasting influence. He "knew that the Father had put all things under his power, and that he had come from God and was returning to God; so he got up from the meal, took off his outer clothing, and wrapped a towel around his waist. After that, he poured water into a basin and began to wash his disciples' feet, drying them with the towel that was wrapped around him" (vs. 3-5). Even though the Father placed all things under Jesus' power, He still chose an act of service instead of lordship.

Let's further develop this point. Jesus is all-powerful; He could easily have required the disciples wash His feet. Instead, He exemplified the difference between having power and having influence. All too often, power is grabbed through forceful, deceptive, or coercive means. Influence is gained through servanthood and shared experience.

Leadership Challenge: Read John 13

Consider the people you currently lead. Do you lord your power over them? Do you deceive or coerce to get your way? Or do you influence through acts of service? Do you roll up your sleeves or sit back and watch the work get done? Spend time in prayer. Ask God what you can do today to swing the pendulum away from power and toward influence. Note the action items God brings to mind.

NOTES

_____

_____

_____

_____

_____

_____

_____

_____

_____

_____

_____

_____

_____

_____

_____

_____

_____

_____

_____

_____

_____

_____

_____

_____

_____

_____

_____

_____

_____

_____

_____

_____

_____

_____

_____

_____

_____

_____

_____

AVOID SECRET PLANS

The prophet answered, "As surely as the Lord lives, whom I serve,
I will not accept a thing." And even though Naaman urged him, he refused.

—2 Kings 5:16

Leaders are regularly tempted to take control and act independently, which can become a big problem when we don't see eye-to-eye with the leader who's in a position over us. We can be tempted to secretly work out another plan or to go behind our leader's back to work an angle in our own favor. Before heading down that road, we should remember that God is always watching, and He's not prone to bless secrecy or trickery.

In 2 Kings 5, a man named Gehazi shows us why employing secrets and tricks are a bad course of action. He was working for the prophet Elisha, who had just healed Naaman, an army commander, of leprosy. Naaman was so thankful that he wanted to repay Elisha in some way. "The prophet answered, 'As surely as the LORD lives, whom I serve, I will not accept a thing.' And even though Naaman urged him, he refused" (v. 16). That's when Gehazi thought differently and tricked Naaman into handing over some valuable gifts.

Was it worth it? No, it was a terrible decision! When Gehazi got back, Elisha confronted him. "'Naaman's leprosy will cling to you and to your descendants forever.' Then Gehazi went from Elisha's presence and his skin was leprous—it had become as white as snow" (v. 27). He lived out his days in exile, a punishment that far outweighed any of the valuable items he took.

Leadership Challenge: Read 2 Kings 5

Prayerfully examine your current projects and plans. Are you secretly working another angle? Are you being dishonest in some way? Does your work ethic harbor a vein of deceit or trickery? It's time to come clean. Make notes and then set appointments in your calendar to address the sin before it further affects the future.

NOTES

_____

_____

_____

_____

_____

_____

_____

_____

_____

_____

_____

Day 14
PRAY THROUGH MEMORIES

I thank my God every time I remember you. In all my prayers for all
of you, I always pray with joy.

—Philippians 1:3-4

On the rare occasion that downtime presents itself, leaders should take the opportunity to reflect on past experiences. Pondering this, we often consider people God used to shape us. Naturally, we wonder where they are and what new experiences they're having. How often do we pray for the people we recall? It's not an automatic behavior, is it? Perhaps it should be.

Paul writes to the Christians of Philippi, "I thank my God every time I remember you. In all my prayers for all of you, I always pray with joy because of your partnership in the gospel from the first day until now, being confident of this, that he who began a good work in you will carry it on to completion until the day of Christ Jesus" (Phil. 1:3-6). It's one thing to fondly remember people who helped us along the way. It's an entirely different state of mind when our memories of them bring us before our Lord, thanking Him for them and petitioning on their behalf.

Think about how the Church would grow and ministries thrive if we embraced the practice of Paul's memory prayers. Think about the relationships that would deepen and possibly last longer that they would have otherwise. Contemplate the miraculous intercession that would take place.

Leadership Challenge: Read Philippians 1

Pay attention to Paul's prayerful words. As you go to prayer, let God guide your thoughts to the people of your past and bring them before the Lord. Remember what they have meant to you and thank God for them. Perhaps make a plan to reach out to a person from your past.

NOTES

_____

_____

_____

_____

_____

_____

_____

_____

_____

_____

_____

_____

_____

_____

_____

_____

_____

_____

_____

_____

_____

_____

_____

_____

_____

_____

_____

_____

_____

_____

_____

_____

_____

_____

_____

_____

_____

_____

_____

_____

_____

Day 15
GROW IN HUMILITY

Because your heart was responsive and you humbled yourself before the Lord when you heard what I have spoken against this place and its people—that they would become a curse and be laid waste—and because you tore your robes and wept in my presence, I also have heard you, declares the Lord.

—2 Kings 22:19

Leaders are a work in progress. As we navigate the struggles and conflicts of leadership, we continually learn and grow—that is, if we are willing to grow! Openness to growth is evidence of humility.

Scripture offers many chronicles of leadership: kings, soldiers, prophets, and priests. Unfortunately, many of them neither started nor ended with humility. Far too many accounts tell of their doing "evil in the eyes of the LORD" (2 Kings 17:2). Thankfully, some "did what was right in the eyes of the LORD" (2 Kings 22:2).

One such king was Josiah, a leader who understood humility and wanted to grow. At a time when Israel was very troubled, Josiah worked to bring the people back to God's law. God responded, "Because your heart was responsive and you humbled yourself before the Lord when you heard what I have spoken against this place and its people—that they would become a curse and laid waste—and because you tore your robes and wept in my presence, I have heard you, declares the LORD" (2 Kings 22:19).

Leadership Challenge: Read 2 Kings 22 and 23

Look carefully at King Josiah's life and leadership. As a leader, are you in a place of humility? Are you willing to grow? Spend time in prayer and repentance. Ask God to give you and your team a fresh start, focused on humility and then note your next steps.

NOTES

_____

_____

_____

_____

_____

_____

_____

_____

_____

_____

_____

_____

_____

_____

_____

_____

Day 16
HAVE PERSONAL MISSION

He is the one we proclaim, admonishing and teaching everyone with
all wisdom, so that we may present everyone fully mature in Christ.

—Colossians 1:28

It is hard to talk about leadership and not reference mission or vision. Some businesses, organizations, churches, and nonprofits have lengthy mission and vision statements. Few of them are memorable. Other organizations do the work to craft concise statements that almost every employee, member, and donor can readily recite. The latter is the one that has staying power.

In Colossians 1, we find a mission statement of sorts. Paul outlines several thoughts in this chapter, but verse twenty-eight seems to encompass his purpose. "He is the one we proclaim, admonishing and teaching everyone with all wisdom, so that we may present everyone fully mature in Christ." This statement focuses on the work of ministry with an eternal perspective. It points the reader to the bigger picture— what Paul truly strives for in his daily efforts of service.

Perhaps your situation is difficult because your organization's drive is profit or another temporal focus that does not align with your personal resolution. Maybe it is long and outdated, but you do not have the influence to make a change. Take heart! The quality of that official statement does not have to guide you personally. Instead, it is time to create a mission statement that is your own.

Leadership Challenge: Read Colossians 1

Meditate on the mission Paul lays out for the Colossian Christians. Spend time in prayer and then start writing. Work to construct a single sentence that encompasses who you are, what you care about, and where you are going. Let this statement drive you, directing every role and responsibility of your life and leadership.

NOTES

_____

_____

_____

_____

_____

_____

_____

_____

_____

_____

_____

_____

_____

_____

_____

_____

_____

_____

_____

_____

_____

_____

_____

_____

_____

_____

_____

_____

_____

_____

_____

_____

_____

_____

_____

_____

_____

_____

_____

_____

Day 17
BUILD SOME FRIENDSHIPS

And the Lord's servant must not be quarrelsome but must be kind to everyone, able to teach, not resentful.

—2 Timothy 2:24

Whether it is a business, church, or nonprofit organization, the workplace can have its fair share of uncomfortable conversations. Too many of these interactions lead to uncomfortable relationships. We begin to avoid certain people or places at specific times, in order to avoid contact. As leaders, we should be above these thoughts and behaviors.

For many years, there was an underlying belief that people should not build relationships within the workplace. The perspective was based on the fear that we may have to fire one of our friends. This philosophy built unapproachability into leadership positions and fostered deeper divides between leaders and team members than the results of having to fire a friend might have.

As Christians, we should lean into kindness and friendship in the workplace. In 2 Timothy 2, Paul tells his apprentice, "Don't have anything to do with foolish and stupid arguments, because you know they produce quarrels . . . be kind to everyone, able to teach, not resentful. Opponents must be gently instructed, in the hope that God will grant them repentance leading them to a knowledge of the truth" (vs. 23-25). What would our careers look like and feel like if we applied this perspective in the workplace each day?

Leadership Challenge: Read 2 Timothy 2

Concentrate on how the principles of kindness and gentleness build friendships. Pray about your work relationships, make notes, and set a few appointments to connect with colleagues you typically ignore or perhaps get on your nerves.

NOTES

_____

_____

_____

_____

_____

_____

_____

_____

_____

_____

_____

_____

_____

_____

Day 18
DREAM WITH SUBMISSION

Trust in the Lord with all your heart and lean not on your own understanding; in all your ways submit to him, and he will make your paths straight.

—Proverbs 3:5-6

Dreams, goals, and aspirations benefit us in many ways; and they connect closely to all forms of leadership. They keep us focused on the tasks at hand and keep us moving in a forward direction. That said, we will experience ups and downs—times when we might have to take a few steps backward. Nevertheless, the hope is that we get a little closer to our ultimate goal, whatever that may be, each day.

Proverbs 3 provides unique leadership principles for staying on track with our goals. The chapter begins as a father speaks, "My son, do not forget my teaching, but keep my commands in your heart, for they will prolong your life many years and bring you peace and prosperity" (vs. 1-2). This idea fits; many dreams and goals accompany or lead to a desire for peace and prosperity. Submitting to the teaching we have been given provides a framework to reach them.

Further down in the chapter, the father continues, "Trust in the LORD with all your heart and lean not on your own understanding; in all your ways submit to him, and he will make your paths straight" (vs. 5-6). A leader's forward path can be full of twists and turns, but trusting in and submitting to the Lord puts us on a straightened path.

Leadership Challenge: Read Proverbs 3

Read each verse in light of aspirations and identify areas in which you lack trust. Then ask God to show you where you have not been fully submitted to Him. As God answers, rewrite your goals with a heart of trust and submission.

NOTES

_____

_____

_____

_____

_____

_____

_____

_____

_____

_____

_____

_____

_____

_____

_____

CHOOSE GOD'S SIDE

"'Go home, every one of you, for this is my doing.'" So they obeyed the word of the Lord and went home again, as the Lord had ordered.

—1 Kings 12:24b

Power struggles happen in leadership. Our desire to keep people on our side can result in a temptation to manipulate. All of a sudden, we neglect integrity and authenticity, replacing them with selfish behaviors. This situation never ends well, but too often, we fall into this trap.

In 1 Kings 12, we see two opposing leaders, Rehoboam and Jeroboam. A battle is about to ensue when Rehoboam receives a message: "Do not go up to fight against your brothers, the Israelites. Go home, every one of you, for this is my doing" (v. 24). He and his army obey the Lord's instruction, turn back, and go home.

On the other side, Jeroboam begins to plot. "The kingdom will now likely revert to the house of David. If these people go up to offer sacrifices at the temple of the Lord in Jerusalem . . . They will kill me and return to King Rehoboam" (vs. 26-27). Instead of seeking God's instruction, he looks to human advisors, who tell him to make golden calves for worship.

Jeroboam builds shrines and appoints priests for the idols, telling the people, "Here are your gods, Israel, who brought you up out of Egypt" (v. 28). They offered sacrifices to the false gods, which became "the sin of the house of Jeroboam that led to its downfall and to its destruction" (13:34).

Leadership Challenge: Read 1 Kings 12 and 13

Pray through your current conflicts. Do you lack integrity and authenticity? Do you go to human advisors instead of God's guidance? It is time to make some changes. Note conversations to be had and actions to be taken that will bring unity to the situation.

NOTES

_____

_____

_____

_____

_____

_____

_____

_____

_____

_____

_____

_____

_____

_____

_____

_____

_____

_____

_____

_____

_____

_____

_____

_____

_____

_____

_____

_____

_____

_____

_____

_____

_____

_____

_____

_____

_____

NURTURE FAMILY TIME

*Fathers, do not exasperate your children; instead, bring them up in
the training and instruction of the Lord.*

—Ephesians 6:4

It is hard to find a leader who does not like to work. From
planning to projects, meetings to management, most leaders love
working. This trait considered, we should be careful that we do not
sacrifice our family for the sake of a job. Regardless of how much
money we bring home, fully providing for one's family means more
than just putting food on the table.

Paul reminds the Ephesian fathers, "Do not exasperate your
children; instead, bring them up in the training and instruction of
the Lord" (Eph. 6:4). This verse is typically applied to parents who are
too harsh to their children. However, choosing to be absent for meals,
family outings, and special events for the sake of work can be equally
exasperating for our families.

If we are called to lead our families with the same passion and
fervency that we lead our ministry or teams at work, we must balance
our time correctly. We must consider Paul's instruction every time we
enter another project or meeting into the calendar. To truly bring our
families into the training and instruction of the Lord, we have to be

present. Being present means fully engaging in the family's activities. The heart and mind must follow the body to the event or activity!

Leadership Challenge: Read Ephesians 6

Recall the past week. Have you fully engaged with your family? Have you spent dedicated time with your spouse and each of your children? Take notes of reflection and set weekly or even daily appointments in the calendar to nurture your family.

NOTES

_____

_____

_____

_____

_____

_____

_____

_____

_____

_____

_____

_____

_____

PRAY FOR LEADERS

I urge, then, first of all, that petitions, prayers, intercession and
thanksgiving be made for all people—for kings and all those in authority.
—1 Timothy 2:1-2a

With all the day-to-day responsibilities a leader carries, it is tough to take a moment and think about the bigger picture. How could our national and international governments affect our leadership? Would we have this position during a time of global or societal struggle? Do we benefit from this time and place? Are we praying about it? Are we thanking God for the massive oversight and provision that occurs, day in and day out, without our even acknowledging it?

First Timothy 2 begins with Paul urging his apprentice, "First of all, that petitions, prayers, intercession and thanksgiving be made for all people—for kings and all those in authority, that we may live peaceful and quiet lives in all godliness and holiness. This is good, and pleases God our Savior, who wants all people to be saved and to come to a knowledge of the truth" (vs. 1-4).

Leaders should show initiative in all areas of our lives. This aim includes daily, if not hourly, prayer. Per Paul's instruction, prayer for national leaders is a critical endeavor! We should consider the stresses of our leadership roles and then contemplate the stress level of people who work on a national or global scale. Regardless of whether we agree with their policies, Scripture clearly indicates that they need our prayer support.

Leadership Challenge: Read 1 Timothy 2

As you read this passage, write principles as God brings them to mind. Pray specifically today for your nation's leaders, whether good or bad. Ask God to intercede in a particular event or simply to provide peace and rest as they labor.

NOTES

_____

_____

_____

_____

_____

_____

_____

_____

_____

_____

_____

_____

_____

Day 22
SEEK GOD'S JUSTICE

Many seek an audience with a ruler,
but it is from the Lord that one gets justice.

—Proverbs 29:26

Throughout history, great leaders have been known to seek justice. When someone has been cheated, hurt, or wronged in some way, great leaders stood beside them and fought on their behalf. Often, this act placed their names in the history books and is why we look to their stories for inspiration.

Today, we may fight for some cause or speak out against a serious problem that everyone else ignores. If we are not being heard, we often look to people above us to take action—the company's CEO, church's pastor, or a politician on a local or national scale. We expect them to do something about the situation. We expect them to find justice for us or the crisis for which we believe they should be fighting.

The author of Proverbs 29 writes, "Many seek an audience with a ruler, but it is from the LORD that one gets justice" (v. 26). Interesting, isn't it? Even if we go to the top dog to get things sorted, it is God Who makes the ultimate judgment. Justice, like everything else in our lives, is purposed through the will of our heavenly Father. We may not understand the plan, but He does. If God felt that a certain manager or politician needed persuading, He could change their mind in a heartbeat. I am not saying we should be silent and let injustice reign. I do suggest, however, that leaders should promote prayer over resistance.

Leadership Challenge: Read Proverbs 29

Take notes on applicable principles in Proverbs. Prayerfully allow God to bring forward the injustices that cause you to struggle. As you note each injustice, submit it to His will and make a conscious choice this week to pray and seek God's plan in the context of each situation.

NOTES

_____

_____

_____

_____

_____

_____

_____

_____

_____

_____

_____

_____

_____

SCHEDULE BREAK TIME

Be wise in the way you act toward outsiders;
make the most of every opportunity.

—Colossians 4:5

Most organizations give employees a few coffee breaks and a lunch break. While the length of each may vary, this practice is pretty standard in the Western world. Unfortunately, many leaders remain in their offices or on the job site, rather than heading to the break room. This habit is a mistake.

In Colossians, Paul tells the Church to "be wise in the way you act toward outsiders; make the most of every opportunity. Let your conversation be always full of grace, seasoned with salt, so that you may know how to answer everyone" (vs. 5-6). Observing these verses in the context of our careers, continuing to work keeps our coworkers and team members as outsiders, limiting Gospel opportunities as well as potential friendships. People are important to God and should be important to us. Locking ourselves in our office or staying on the job site when everyone goes out for lunch just to squeeze in ten more minutes of work does not seem like the best decision from a relational or eternal perspective.

Alternatively, engaging in conversation over coffee or lunch shows authenticity. After all, leaders are real people, too! More importantly, from a Christ-centered perspective, it shows that we care about the people around us. We may just receive an opportunity to build a friendship and share the Gospel.

Leadership Challenge: Read Colossians 4

Consider the character to which Paul calls the Colossians. Honestly and prayerfully think through the past month and make a tally of the times you took a break with your colleagues. Note the levels of grace and saltiness of those breaktime conversations. Then take out your calendar and schedule intentional breaks with your team this week.

NOTES

_____

_____

_____

_____

_____

_____

_____

_____

_____

_____

Day 24
PRIORITIZE SOME REST

In vain you rise early and stay up late, toiling for food to eat—
for he grants sleep to those he loves.

—Psalm 127:2

It starts with a sneeze, a cough, or maybe just a tickle in the back of your throat. Then the paranoia appears because you can feel you are about to get sick. Your leadership is about to be undermined by something you cannot even see. Regret sets in. For the sake of work, you have not been taking care of yourself. More importantly, busy days and late nights prevented you from getting the rest your body craves. Now, your body is going to make you rest!

The psalmist writes that "unless the Lord builds the house, the builders labor in vain. Unless the Lord watches over the city, the guards stand watch in vain. In vain you rise early and stay up late, toiling for food to eat—for he grants sleep to those he loves" (Psalm 127:1-2). God issued a day of rest for a reason. He provided a sabbath day for our benefit, but too often, we ignore it. Under the New Covenant, we are no longer under the law of the Sabbath, but that does not mean that we should ignore it.

If we are not making time to eat properly, exercise, or sleep, we are likely neglecting our spiritual needs as well. Soon enough, we are building our house of leadership in vain. At that point, a great way for God to get our attention is to allow an illness to take over, like a forced Sabbath. Once we are in despair, we have no choice but to rest and refocus on our Lord.

Leadership Challenge: Read Psalm 127

Consider the past week or month. How have you been feeling? Are you sleeping well? Have you been taking a day of rest to focus on the Lord, your family, and your health? If not, what prevents that from happening? As you go to prayer, open your calendar and commit to remove a few scheduled items in order to make rest a priority this week.

NOTES

_____

_____

_____

_____

_____

_____

_____

_____

_____

_____

_____

Day 25
OFFER UP THANKSGIVING

Rejoice always, pray continually, give thanks in all circumstances;
for this is God's will for you in Christ Jesus.

—1 Thessalonians 5:16-18

The workload is ominous; the days are long; and the responsibilities seem endless. Such is the life of a leader. Around every corner is a new obstacle or opportunity. We wonder how we are going to fit this new scenario into an already busy life; nonetheless, we must embrace our role and be thankful for the privilege to lead.

In 1 Thessalonians, we find a few short verses with great encouragement to "rejoice always, pray continually, give thanks in all circumstances; for this is God's will for you in Christ Jesus" (5:16-18). Regardless of the mountains we have to climb, God is in control. Assuming we are caring for our physical, mental, emotional, and spiritual health, we can overcome any obstacle and champion any opportunity.

Some days, though, we feel we cannot overcome the obstacle nor champion the cause set before us. This time is when we must pause, rejoice, go to prayer, and be thankful. It may feel like a trivial task. Too often, leaders are wired to push through in our own strength, even though intellectually, we know it is a resource in short supply. Instead, let us embrace our seemingly trivial rejoicing and thanksgiving, knowing that they reverberate into eternity and that our ever-watchful God sustains us when the load is beyond our control.

Leadership Challenge: Read 1 Thessalonians 5

Take in these words of encouragement and write down each principle that applies to your current work or ministry. Pray through each principle, asking God to bring you into that place of rejoicing and thanksgiving. Give God the many thanks that He deserves for blessing you with the opportunity to lead.

NOTES

_____

_____

_____

_____

_____

_____

_____

_____

_____

_____

_____

_____

Day 26
EMBRACE LIFE'S CHANGE

There is a time for everything,
and a season for every activity under the heavens.

—Ecclesiastes 3:1

For most leaders, life is good when each day rolls along according to schedule. Every once in a while, we get gifts like waking up ten minutes before the alarm, finishing a project before its deadline, or attending a meeting that ends early. On the other end of the spectrum, we also run into the challenges of change—like when we forget to set the alarm, the project hits roadblocks, or that meeting is dragging on *forever*!

Ecclesiastes reminds us that "there is a time for everything, and a season for every activity under the heavens" (3:1). Following this statement, the author gives a plethora of examples of how life can bring seasons of change to our lives. This alteration should not cause us anxiety or alarm; instead, we should embrace life's changes as opportunities to grow.

When it comes right down to it, change is really a marker of what it means to be in leadership. Setting leaders apart from the average worker is the ability to stay focused and motivated amid seasons of change. Do not get me wrong. Times of illness and mourning hinder even the strongest leader—and they should. Encountering these seasons is part of the human experience. We lean on God to overcome and grow though them.

Leadership Challenge: Read Ecclesiastes 3

Prayerfully focus on each season of life mentioned in this passage. Where are you currently? Is life moving along flawlessly, or are you in a season of change? Is a season of difficult change on the horizon? How will you act, think, speak, and motivate others during this season? Note how you will embrace life's changes this week.

NOTES

_____

_____

_____

_____

_____

_____

_____

_____

_____

_____

_____

_____

_____

LEARN FROM CRITICISM

As iron sharpens iron, so one person sharpens another.

—Proverbs 27:17

It is tough to take criticism, particularly when we feel like our motives are being attacked. For leaders, it comes with the territory to have our thoughts and ideas questioned. Soon enough, someone will question whether our character is steadfast and honorable.

In the book of Proverbs, we see a small-yet-powerful verse that many a leader has quoted. "As iron sharpens iron, so one person sharpens another" (Prov. 27:17). As we are challenged by people around us, we are sharpened. As a result, we become more prepared for the next dispute or confrontation. It does not always feel good, but most people do mean well. Even having our character questioned or criticized may hurt, but it could point to an area of struggle in our lives that needs to be addressed.

While these ideas hold truth, receiving criticism is difficult, especially when it is not constructively delivered. However, we can choose to accept the rebuke and place ourselves under the sharpening stone once again. As we do, we should constantly remind ourselves that any rebuke, criticism, or questioning of character provides growth for a leader. We will get a sharper edge from it!

Leadership Challenge: Read Proverbs 27

Consider the challenges that Proverbs describes and compare them to what you currently face. Note current situations in which your character has been called into question. Write the reason why that criticism hurts, and as you go to prayer, ask God to show you what to learn from that criticism and where to change perspective or behavior.

NOTES

_____

_____

_____

_____

_____

_____

_____

_____

_____

_____

_____

_____

_____

_____

_____

_____

_____

_____

_____

WORK FOR CHRIST

Whatever you do, work at it with all your heart, as working for the Lord,
not for human masters, since you know that you will receive an inheritance
from the Lord as a reward. It is the Lord Christ you are serving.

—Colossians 3:23-24

The temptation is always there. We are supposed to be working on a specific project, but we are checking our inbox or social media for the third time. Worse, we have moved to something not remotely work-related, like a hilarious social media video. This kind of poor leadership can become habitual, leading to a lack of vision and motivation and eventual unemployment.

In Colossians, Paul writes to Christian slaves about their earthly masters. "Whatever you do, work at it with all your heart, as working for the Lord, not for human masters, since you know that you will receive an inheritance from the Lord as a reward. It is the Lord Christ you are serving" (Col. 3:23-24). Though this instruction is written to slaves, its principles hold great value for leaders who live and work in modern-day society.

We ought to perform our careers to the best of our ability. This standard conveys more than simple good ethics; it sets a good example for people we lead, and it applies even during those moments when no one else is around to watch what we do, such as those times when we could leave without anyone else's knowledge. We should have a heavenly mindset during our workday, realizing that our service at work is received as service to Christ.

Leadership Challenge: Read Colossians 3

Spend some time in prayer over this passage. Ask God to convict you, reminding you of times when you may have been lazy and distracted this week. Note each situation as the Lord brings it to mind and determine which tasks you tried to avoid. Then create a to-do list that prioritizes those items. Work diligently at them, as if you were serving Christ directly.

NOTES

_____

_____

_____

_____

_____

_____

_____

_____

_____

_____

SHOW SOME COMPASSION

When he saw the crowds, he had compassion on them,
because they were harassed and helpless, like sheep without a shepherd.
—Matthew 9:36

Leaders are known for their ability to push through any obstacle: pulling all-nighters to complete a project; never taking a sick day; showing up for work, regardless of health; keeping personal loss a secret, despite the pain. Unfortunately, too many of us wear these attributes as badges of honor, but they demonstrate poor leadership, plain and simple.

The situation gets worse when we start expecting this type of unhealthy work ethic from the people on our team. It shows a lack of respect and a lack of compassion. Matthew describes the opposite attitude in Jesus. "When he saw the crowds, he had compassion on them, because they were harassed and helpless, like sheep without a shepherd" (Matt. 9:36). This account is not the only time Jesus was moved with compassion for others.

In Matthew 14, we read of His compassion for the sick. Matthew 20 tells of His compassion for the blind. Luke 7 discusses His compassion for a woman whose son had died. The list can continue!

Surely, all leaders who desire to follow Jesus should be marked by some level of compassion.

When you look over your team, do you feel any compassion? When someone calls in sick or has a personal crisis, do you release them and then pray for them? Faithful leaders leave the details in the Lord's hands, instead of policing time off or assessing the excuse's validity. Faithful leaders risk being seen as a pushover in order to be compassionate.

Leadership Challenge: Read Matthew 9

Pay attention to the compassion that flows through Christ's leadership. As you pray, think about your leadership and how you have treated your staff in recent months. Pull out your calendar and set appointments to speak with your team members, apologizing when appropriate. Make a fresh start as a compassionate leader.

NOTES

_____

_____

_____

_____

_____

_____

_____

_____

_____

Day 30
BECOME A BIBLICAL LEADER

Be on your guard; stand firm in the faith; be courageous;
be strong. Do everything in love.

—1 Corinthians 16:13-14

It is easy for life to become routine, letting each day pass like the next one. If we let it, the routine can weaken our defense against sin, keep us from studying Scripture, soften our desire to share the Gospel, and prevent us from showing Christ's love. As leaders, we should find a higher calling than the weekly routine and a greater vision than a job description. If you have worked your way through this book, you are headed in the right direction. Well done!

Paul writes in 1 Corinthians, "Be on your guard; stand firm in the faith; be courageous; be strong. Do everything in love" (16:13-14). All of us can move through life, letting each day come as it will. It takes effort to be on guard against temptation, to stand firm in faith and courage. It takes even more effort to do everything in love. This job description is not one of an average person's strolling through a daily routine. It is a call for the biblical leader.

Leadership can be proven through faithfulness in particular areas. Perhaps we have completed a task or project with excellence, or we are competent and trustworthy, so people follow us. Maybe we have a huge influence on social media through books or large speaking engagements. None of these situations compares to the higher standard for leadership: to be brave and steadfast in our faith and love.

Leadership Challenge: Read 1 Corinthians 16

After reading the passage, prayerfully write down the answers to these questions:

- Do I guard against temptation?
- Do I stand firm in my faith?
- Am I courageous and strong in my convictions?
- Do I accomplish everything in love?

Ask God to help you set five goals to implement these principles in your life. They are your final components of starting to become a biblical leader.

NOTES

_____

_____

_____

_____

_____

_____

_____

_____

STRIVING TO LEAD BIBLICALLY

It is my conviction that Jesus is the Compass and the Bible is the map needed to direct us to God's plan for our future. This belief makes embracing a biblical life and leadership critical and is why I created my website, LeadBiblically.com. With a few clicks, you will find a wealth of biblical insight and useful resources. I strive to post at least once each week. Most content stems from a Christian worldview and contains many reference links to scriptural principles. You will also find a fair share of my own life experience, as I strive to become the leader God has called me to be.

I have not taken the most direct career path. I have participated in both business and ministry worlds during my education and professional experience. I do not believe this happened by mistake. God meshed these two paths to help me better understand and lead people. In addition to helping people find God's call for their lives, I feel a significant burden to encourage smaller churches in smaller communities. If you are in a ministry or nonprofit that feels stuck but want to reach your town or city with the Gospel, please drop me a message at jeremy@leadbiblically.com. If you are looking for affordable training for your team or you would like me to speak at your event or retreat, you will find several options under the Workshops & Retreats menu on my website.

I live in Whitehorse, Canada, where I serve as the lead pastor with Mountainview Church; I am an avid outdoorsman, enjoying a subsistence lifestyle of hunting and fishing for food, eating everything we harvest. Living in the North provides ample opportunity to access God's blessing of the wild and vast creation. I am a podcast and audiobook junkie. I enjoy using Apple devices and have been known to dabble in video editing. I am an average guitar player and vocalist. And no matter what I am doing, coffee is a staple; from lattes to gas station joe, I will drink it!

It is important to remember that biblical leadership begins at home. I need to cherish my time with my wife, Nicole, and our three boys: Jude, Luke, and Mark. Engaging in an outdoor activity with them often becomes the most memorable family time. Spending time in God's creation refreshes us as a family, so we try to engage in a variety of outdoor seasonal pursuits. Some days, though, nothing is better than a sabbath time of rest—like a family movie night for the five of us, snuggled on the couch with a big bowl of popcorn.

Let's connect! Feel free to send me a message at jeremy@leadbiblically.com or call my cell at 867-335-7524 anytime. We can also schedule a Zoom or FaceTime call. For locals, I would be more than willing to grab a coffee. People who prefer to connect through social media are welcome to choose one of the following platforms.

- TikTik/PastorJeremyNorton
- Twitter/PastorJNorton
- Facebook.com/PastorJeremyNorton
- Instagram.com/PastorJeremyNorton
- LinkedIn.com/In/PastorJeremyNorton

I look forward to interacting with you. Enjoy browsing LeadBiblically.com. Thanks for joining me on this journey of growth, serving Christ by cultivating biblical leadership!

In His Service,

Jeremy Norton

Disclaimer: The thoughts and opinions shared in this book do not necessarily represent those of Mountainview Church.

More from Ambassador International

There is a desperate need for effective leadership today: in our nation, in our churches, in our families, and even in ourselves. The Bible uses the term *armorbearer* to describe leaders who offer help, support and strength to those around them. Packed with inspiring stories and powerful lessons, *Armorbearers* reveals the four revolutionary choices every leader must make, risking their own significance in order to encounter God in life-altering ways. Are you ready to become an armorbearer?

There are many different types of leaders— leaders in the business world, in government, in the home, and in the local church. Sadly, many leaders are focused on what they can get from their position rather than on what they can give. While some view it as a tool for popularity and power, leadership is a privilege and it requires responsibility. We need biblical leaders who are people of integrity and humility—leaders who are willing to be different.

The devotions in *Called to Lead* are written for workplace leaders who are looking for something solid to help you improve your leadership. If you are looking for a devotional to simply warm your heart or cram more Scripture between your ears, find another book. If you are eager to close the gap between the leader you are and the leader God created you to be, humble enough to recognize you could use some help, and willing to try a proven approach, invest a few minutes each week with this book pondering the intersection of your life and leadership and God's Word.

Made in the USA
Monee, IL
06 November 2023

45871289R00079